Hawai'i

The Past Fifty Years · The Next Fifty Years

Hawai'i

THE PAST FIFTY YEARS • THE NEXT FIFTY YEARS

By George R. Ariyoshi

Governor of Hawai'i, 1973-1986

The author wishes to thank Duane Kurisu for partnering on this project;
George Engebretson and Watermark Publishing for production and distribution services;
Neida Bangerter of the Maui Arts & Cultural Center; Shuhei Abe,
Michael Shimoko and Dr. Lawrence Tseu for their support; and Tom Coffman
for his assistance in research and editing.

ISBN 978-0-9821698-9-6

Design and production
Gonzalez Design

Photography
Tom Coffman and the Hawai‘i State Archives

Watermark Publishing
1088 Bishop St., Suite 310
Honolulu, Hawai‘i 96813
Telephone 1-808-587-7766
Toll-free 1-866-900-BOOK
sales@bookshawaii.net
www.bookshawaii.net

Printed in the United States

Portraits of Hawai‘i's people, included on the covers and page 2
with the kind permission of the artists, are from the Schaefer Portrait
Challenge exhibition organized and presented by
the Maui Arts & Cultural Center.

Page 2 (clockwise from left):

Kathy Ostman-Magnusen: *Mr. Magnusen*

Judy Kerstetter: *Hideo Ishigo, Honomu Baker*

Douglas Ball: *Little Dancer*

Stephen Garnin: *Benny Deluna*

Albert Weight: *Dad*

Jill Butterbaugh: *Kimo: Ha‘aheo*

Roger B. Stevens: *I'd Rather Be Dreaming*

Mike Carroll: *Alberta de Jetley, Farmer*

Mitsuhiro Kuwahara: *Gina 1*

Wendy Romanchak (center): *Liam*

Contents

The Constitution of the State of Hawaii

Where Have We Been?

Where Do We Go from Here?

To Rebecca
Aloha
George R Ariyoshi

The state of Hawai'i's 50th anniversary is an opportunity to think about both past and future. "Where have we been?" leads us to "Where do we go from here?"

If we have an understanding of the past, we can make better choices about the future. By training our minds to think across the generations, we can improve our own lives and those of our children and grandchildren.

In the early years of statehood, we the people of Hawai'i enjoyed a wide agreement about the direction we wanted to go. Now we are more scattered. My hope is to share turning points in our history while mapping the challenges we face. I hope to be educational. It's my way of saying, "Okay, young people. It's your turn. You can't take the good life for granted, so let's get to work. The future belongs to you."

George R. Ariyoshi
Governor of Hawai'i, 1973-1986

Democracy from the Bottom Up

Step one, democracy cannot be taken for granted. We who came of age before statehood worked to build a democracy from the bottom up.

My high school principal, Dr. Miles E. Cary, practiced John Dewey's philosophy of progressive education. Under the sway of his perpetually optimistic spirit, McKinley High School was an enclave of impassioned democracy surrounded by a hierarchical plantation society. If the plantations tended to say, "No you can't," we said, "Yes we can." Each of us had a handbook called "How May I Participate Intelligently in McKinley High School?"

The handbook proclaimed, "McKinley's whole program is based upon the idea of democracy." In homeroom we discussed issues of the school. We elected a chair who served in the Representative Assembly. The Executive Councils of the sophomore, junior and senior classes formed the Student Council, which made policy on school programs. We had a safety board, a court, police officers and a police commission.

I worked as a student reporter on the daily newspaper, the *Pinion*. We were encouraged to speak our minds. Although I had suffered as a boy from a speech impediment, I improved sufficiently to participate in oratorical contests at McKinley and went on to be a college debater. Each of us was encouraged to help the community in some way outside of school. The handbook told us, "Study your laws, help make better ones, and when you are through school, take your part in the community and see that the laws do what they are supposed to do in a democracy."

In 1935 and 1937, U.S. congressional committees created exitement by holding hearings on statehood for Hawai'i. The crowd peeks into Iolani Palace.

8

When the Bombs Fell

On December 7, 1941, Japan bombed Pearl Harbor, midway through my sophomore year. My grandchildren are amazed when I tell them that during all my high school years, I never went out at night! No dates. No dances. We had a 6:00 p.m. curfew. We sat inside our closed blinds, obeying the martial law blackout. Once a month, we worked in the pineapple fields to make up the labor shortage.

Traditional leaders of the Japanese community deemed "too close to Japan" were taken into custody. The partial self-government of the Territory of Hawai'i was suspended, and the Army ruled. Everything was regulated. Goods were rationed. Constitutional rights went out the window.

My senior year, 1944, I was invited to conferences of adults who were dedicated to building the future of Hawai'i. The theme was how to create a postwar society in which everyone was an active participant regardless of race, creed or color. The idea of statehood for Hawai'i was never far from our minds. We equated it with first-class citizenship.

Japan's attack on Pearl Harbor on Dec. 7, 1941, threw Hawai'i into a crisis that strengthened our claim to statehood.

Article 1, Section 5. No person shall be deprived of life, liberty or property without due process of law, nor be denied the equal protection of the laws, nor be denied the enjoyment of the person's civil rights or be discriminated against in the exercise thereof because of race, religion, sex or ancestry.

People signed a petition that ran all the way up Bishop Street.
A theme was "We are 100% American. And we proved it."

The Arrival of Statehood

I think you see why most of us greeted statehood enthusiastically. The public referendum (yes or no) approved statehood by a margin of 17 to one. The celebration was exuberant.

We had earned our way and paid a price. We had suffered the attack on Pearl Harbor. Our soldiers sacrificed themselves and proved their loyalty to America.

After the war, an elected constitutional convention wrote the progressive draft Constitution of 1950, which was aimed at showing what kind of state we could be. A new wave of young Territorial legislators won office in 1954.

During this exciting period, I was the youngest legislator (which helps explain why I am still here). The core concepts of Hawai'i were fair play, tolerance, equal opportunity and education for all. We were in control of our own destiny. Our governor was elected by our people, not appointed by Washington. Similarly, our judges were chosen by our own people, not Washington. We sent our own senators and representatives to Congress. All in all, statehood felt like a big wave of change.

The Statehood Boom, 1959-1970

Suddenly Hawai'i was on everyone's map. Hawai'i was in movies and books. People the world over wanted to come here. Americans craved to see the new state. The large jets came on line almost exactly with statehood, and tourism began its dramatic rise. The old tourism for the wealthy few—the tourism of the Royal Hawaiian Hotel—gave way to travel for the many. In the first year of statehood, the number of visitors increased by 40 percent.

With ever-greater frequency, we in Hawai'i got out to explore the country of which we were now a first-class part. In the process, we discovered that if you were from Hawai'i, you were the object of envy. Being from Hawai'i gave you a kind of celebrity status.

On the opposite side of the ocean, Japan was recovering from World War II. With the rising importance of Asia, we began to talk about an Age of the Pacific.

Working Together through Government

Around 1970, the public mood changed substantially. We liked the economic growth, and we liked our full participation in the democratic process. But we were caught up in a reaction to the rapid development and urbanization that came with statehood. On a broader front, protests of planetary degradation led to the first Earth Day in 1970. The first major oil crisis hit us in 1973. Native Hawaiians increasingly raised issues related to the overthrow of the Hawaiian Kingdom, annexation by the United States and dispossession from their traditional land base.

The Vietnam War continued through those years, dividing us politically and emotionally. Turmoil and dissension reverberated around the country. Voters nationally pulled back into a state of reaction; the leadership of the United States passed from Presidents Kennedy and Johnson to President Nixon.

By then I had served in the Legislature 16 years. In 1970 I was elected lieutenant governor on the ticket of a large figure in our history, Gov. John A. Burns. I became acting governor in 1973, and the next year I was proud and humbled to be elected the first nonwhite governor of an American state.

I fervently hoped that we in Hawai'i could resolve the divisions that were descending upon us. We had to shape events rather than merely react. We had to talk with one another, sometimes when our views differed greatly.

While many people across the country came to see government as the problem, we in Hawai'i affirmed the idea of working together through the state government. I think it is important to reflect on the fact that because of the self-government enabled by statehood, we remained a progressive society.

The Hawai'i State Plan

We generated new ideas. We stabilized the environment, which is why we still have the relatively clean air, water and beaches that we have today. We asserted greater control over our resources—land, water, agriculture, historic sites, cultural sites, open spaces and the surrounding oceans.

We broadened our commitments to social justice. In 1974 the Legislature passed and I signed into law the first and only mandatory prepaid health insurance act in an American state. At the time we took great pride in being first in the country on many social issues.

My job during my time as governor (1973-1986) was to stimulate thinking and to nurture wide ownership of the best ideas. The public dialogue always began with a reminder of our shared affection for Hawai'i. I must have said it hundreds of times, but believed it with my heart each time: Hawai'i is a special place.

In response to the rapid growth of population and rapid changes in the landscape, I assembled a task force and asked them to think in new ways. We dealt with fundamental questions: What would the long-term impacts of rapid growth be? Growth for whom? Growth to what end? What was the carrying capacity of our fragile environment?

We could not talk about a year or two years from now, but 10, 20 or 30 years. What kind of place would we leave for our children and grandchildren? I tried to make everyone keenly aware that unless we planned effectively, we would fail in our obligation to future generations. We focused on our most basic resources: people, land, water and air.

My task force generated a conscious policy of managed growth that became the Hawai'i State Plan. The goal was not zero growth but moderate, incremental growth that nurtured society's definable objectives. Survey research for the Plan showed the public supported managed-growth policies by astonishing margins, often on the order of nine to one. In retrospect I think we can see the State Plan was a first cut at the idea of sustainability. It anticipated thinking that more recently has gone around the globe.

The 1978 State Constitution

Many of the broader planning concepts of the State Plan were embedded in the 1978 revisions to Hawai'i's constitution. I grant you that constitutions make tough reading, so I've tried to share excerpts from our constitution through these pages. Our constitution is visionary. I hope you can get a flavor of its lofty goals. (See the entire document at http://hawaii.gov/lrb/con/)

Article 11, Section 1. For the benefit of present and future generations, the State and its political subdivisions shall conserve and protect Hawai'i's natural beauty and all natural resources, including land, water, air, minerals and energy sources resources … All public natural resources are held in trust by the State for the benefit of the people.

Article 11, Section 9. Each person has the right to a clean and healthful environment… Any person may enforce this right against any party, public or private, through appropriate legal proceedings, subject to reasonable limitations and regulation as provided by law.

Re-examining the State of Hawai'i

Let's be honest. As we observe 50 years of Hawai'i statehood, the tradition I'm describing—the core belief in the power of government to address problems—has declined. The traditional leadership in not only government but also business and labor has weakened. Key institutions have deteriorated. Our planning processes have been undercut.

We are still thought of as special, but Hawai'i occupies a less distinctive niche in the national and world stage than it did. We are less sure of what Hawai'i has to offer. We are less in touch with what makes us different.

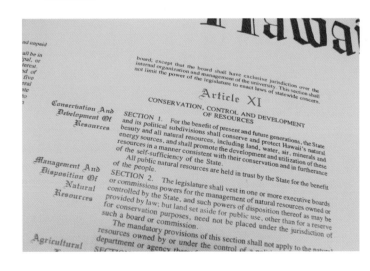

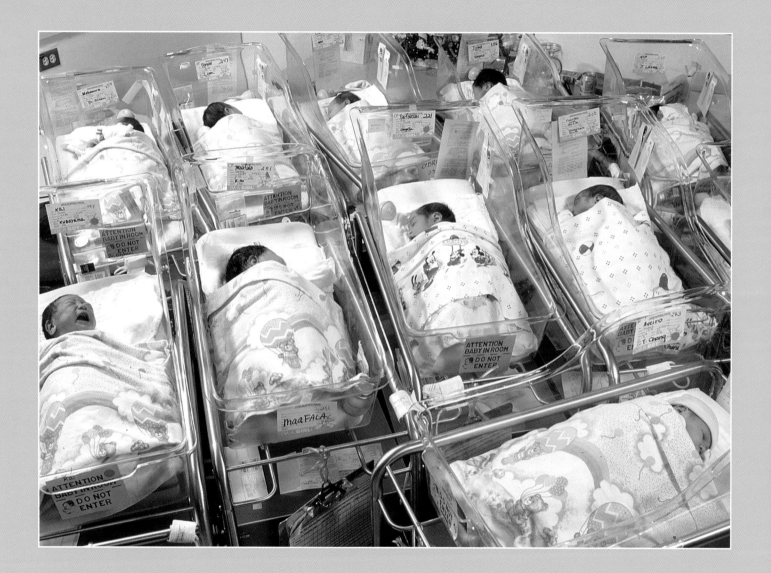

Sustainability +

In recent years, sustainability has been advanced as an idea around which we can organize our efforts. The 1987 report *Our Common Future* said, "Sustainable development is development that meets the needs of the present without compromising the ability of future generations to meet their own needs." Sustainability became the guiding concept of the First Earth Summit in 1992. As such the sustainability movement was rooted in the global environmental movement, with an emphasis on meeting the needs of the world's poor. It was adapted in Hawai'i as the core concept of the Hawai'i 2050 Plan by the 2008 Hawai'i Legislature.

I was recruited off the shelf to serve as one of the speakers at the 2050 conference. I talked about the need to think in terms not only of a year or several years but of generations. I listened carefully to what young people had to say. I most remember the high school students who talked about how they love Hawai'i but doubt they will live here, either for lack of career opportunity or lack of housing. Their comments starkly framed the issues of sustainability.

I went away thinking that if sustainability is to serve as our rallying cry, let's sharpen it. To achieve sustainability we must think as good stewards. We must use the democratically shared powers of government to shape the future through a participatory and open process. That means respecting diverse views and being open to a constantly changing world while acting as conservers of public funds and resources.

We can't do everything we might like to do. Therefore we need effective government that is based on an educated electorate. Underlying this electorate must be a strong sense that we are all in this project together, and that we all hold a stake in what makes Hawai'i special.

I suggest that sustainability is a starting point, but we need Sustainability + Something. The theme for the plus can only arise from a revitalized public life. Young people must develop their own statement about what is special about Hawai'i.

"How to bring into being a world that is not only sustainable, functional and equitable but also deeply desirable is a question of leadership and ethics and vision and courage, properties not of computer models but of the human heart and soul."

—Donella & Dennis Meadows and Jorgen Randers, *Limits to Growth*

Hawai'i's People

It is beyond our power to control everything, but assessing trends will strengthen our hand in shaping the future.

As America's only island state, we have been especially population-conscious. Generally, we have expressed a preference for a slow population growth over a rapid population growth. The concept of managing population growth is embedded in our constitution, but we have constrained ourselves (and been constrained by federal court rulings) from pursuing this idea in the law.

Total Population

Our population has more than doubled in 50 years.

State of Hawai'i	1959	2007	Projected 2035
All Islands	622,000	1.3 million	1.6 million

As the reaction to rapid population growth set in, the historian Gavan Daws wrote, "(We) are an island community gone mad, behaving like a limitless continent in a world that has already turned into a crowded, strained island." The rate of growth was thought to be unsustainable at about 2.4 percent a year (hence, triple the national average). In the 1980s, the annual rate of population growth slowed to about 1.5 percent, at least partly due to managed growth policies.

With prolonged economic stagnation during the 1990s, Hawai'i was one of only a few states to experience a net loss of population. In the past decade, the growth rate has hovered between one-half and one percent.

Geographic Distribution

At the beginning of statehood, eight out of 10 people lived on O'ahu. The islands of Hawai'i, Maui and Kaua'i had only 132,000 people. The Neighbor Islands were dotted with plantation camps that had been abandoned and plantation towns that were drying up. With a major assist from State government, the Neighbor Islands were revitalized, so the complaint today is "Too many people. Too much traffic."

These are the 50-year changes:

Island/County	1959	2007	% change
O'ahu	489,919	905,601	+85%
Hawai'i	60,658	173,057	+185%
Kaua'i	28,369	62,828	+121%
Maui	43,141	141,902	+229%

Composition

The Hawai'i of 1959 was most often described as a melting pot. As continued evidence of this influential image, people of mixed ancestry today are the fastest growing group.

However, during the statehood years, much thought and energy has gone into perpetuating and celebrating ethnic cultures. As modification of the melting pot image, I conjured the idea of a mixed stew. The flavors run together but the bites retain their character.

People have commemorated their ethnic cultures in exciting ways. None has had such a far-reaching effect as the Native Hawaiian renaissance, which took flight during the 1970s and continues today.

Ethnic Changes

When Hawai'i became a state, people of Japanese ancestry were the largest ethnic group. Seeking to overcome prejudice and discrimination, Japanese Americans played a leading role in establishing the state of Hawai'i.

With statehood, Caucasians began migrating to Hawai'i in large numbers. During the 1980s, Caucasians surpassed Japanese as Hawai'i's largest ethnic group. Although Caucasians today are the largest group, the Caucasian population has increased more slowly than many people expected in 1959.

Immigration into the U.S. from foreign countries became "color-blind" in 1965, thanks in part to the national influence of Hawai'i's newly elected congressional delegation. As a result, the greatly increased migration from Asia has expanded pre-existing groups (such as Filipinos, Koreans and Chinese) and allowed for the development of new ones (such as Vietnamese and Cambodians). The number of Hispanics also has risen sharply. In the year of statehood, just over a thousand people became naturalized citizens. This has reached as high as 6,000 a year in the years since.

The greatest census confusion revolves around the identification of Native Hawaiians. Depending on the definition of Hawaiian and part-Hawaiian, native peoples range between nine and 22 percent. However this category is defined, it appears that the Hawaiian/part-Hawaiian population has not increased, despite a resurgence of Hawaiian culture. On the contrary, it appears that out-migration due to economic reasons recently has resulted in a small net decline of Hawaiians.

A Community of Migrants

As a result of newcomers arriving and local-born people leaving, the idea of a Hawai'i community has changed. The number of those born elsewhere has surpassed the number of local-born.

An Aging Population

When we became a state, an amazing 55 percent of our population was under 25 years old. Today that age group is at one third of the population and falling. Only six percent of the people were over 60 at statehood; today that number has tripled. The percentage of people in the prime taxpayer/breadwinner age group, 25 to 59, peaked in the year 2000 and is waning. By 2035, it is estimated that 27 percent of the population will be over age 60.

Year	Under 25	Age 25-59	Over 60
1960	56%	38%	6%
1980	43%	36%	11%
2000	34%	49%	17%
2035	31%	42%	27%

The relative youth of our 1959 population had its costs in the construction of new schools, a rapidly growing education budget and other services for the young. The aging of Hawai'i's people will have its increased costs in such areas as medical care and long-term care.

Changes in population impact virtually everything we do. One of the obvious areas is use of our land.

Article 9, Section 6. The State and its political subdivisions, as provided by general law, shall plan and manage the growth of the population to protect and preserve the public health and welfare...

The Hawai'i Land Use Law

At the beginning of statehood, our system of land management was the envy of other governmental jurisdictions. We were on the leading edge of land use planning. Delegations periodically arrived to study our land use law. We imagined that as other governments came to see the negative effects of unplanned development, they would emulate us.

As statehood and the jet airplane drove the booming 1960s and 1970s, it was fortunate for Hawai'i that the 1959 Land Use Law was in place. We owe the relative compactness of most urban development in Hawai'i to the Land Use Law, as well as the preservation of much of our agricultural land, scenic vistas, forests and watersheds. Despite our mistakes, our landscape is much more orderly than the sprawling development so often seen in the continental United States.

Originally the job of the land use commissioners was to serve the broad public interest over the long term. When I came into office, I appointed a representative of the League of Women Voters to the commission, because the League had worked hard on understanding land use decisions. I also appointed a young Hawaiian activist who spoke eloquently from a Hawaiian cultural viewpoint about the land; I felt her views needed to be represented. Combined with all we were doing in related areas—for example, in water management—the average annual rezoning of land to urban use was cut in half.

Today the intent and functioning of the Land Use Law has been extensively subverted. The commission membership prominently includes a realtor, a development lawyer and a corporate lawyer. Members with large constituencies are similarly tied to development (such as electrical contractors and the carpenters' union). The commission's executive director previously headed the Land Use Research Foundation, a lobbying group for developers and large landowners.

The decisions of the Land Use Commission to urbanize go a long way toward explaining why the number of construction workers in Hawai'i has doubled in the past decade, and why the general public is increasingly disturbed by the congestion that results from overly rapid development.

Contrary to the original idea of the Land Use Law, the public is substantially shut out of the process. The commission's quasi-judicial proceedings, intended to elicit thoughtful and well-informed testimony, have limited participation to only those with a direct interest in the outcome. Attorneys examine, cross-examine and redirect the examination of witnesses as if in a court of law. Developers seeking rezoning arrive with attorneys, consultants and expert witnesses to pursue their agenda, but the public interest is not represented.

Actual Use of the Land

The most widely embraced goal of the Land Use Law was the preservation of prime agricultural land. The collapse of plantation agriculture is at the heart of our confusion about how to manage land today. The 1978 Constitutional Convention mandated protection of agriculturally important lands, but this mandate has not been satisfactorily implemented.

In the absence of agreement over a land use management system, protection of agricultural, scenic, watershed, historic and cultural lands has weakened.

- Should we allow development of prime agricultural land?

- Should we plant forests on it?

- Can alternative energy crops take up the slack?

- Are these lands actually available for agriculture and, if so, is diversified agriculture putting them to use?

- If diversified agriculture is not using a substantial part of this land, what is its potential otherwise? If diversified agriculture cannot take up the slack, what should we do?

- Are "gentlemen farms" an answer to the land use issue, or are they merely a way around the Land Use Law?

Article 11, Section 3. The State shall conserve and protect agricultural lands, promote diversified agriculture, increase agricultural self-sufficiency and assure the availability of agriculturally suitable lands. The legislature shall provide standards and criteria to accomplish the foregoing lands identified by the State as important agricultural lands needed to fulfill the purposes above shall not be reclassified by the State or rezoned by its political subdivisions without meeting the standards and criteria established by the legislature and approved by a two-thirds vote of the body responsible for the reclassification or rezoning action.

Diversified Agriculture

We should be doing all we can to diversify agriculture, but we are not. The lax administration of agricultural zoning has put pressure on land costs. Also, as farmers get older they begin to see land as a sort of retirement commodity, leading to proposals for development of farmland.

Because of Hawai'i's high land values and the constant temptation of development, I concluded as governor that land must be continuously available to new generations of farmers at agricultural rates. I decided that diversified agriculture needed government-owned lands that can be leased for long terms.

In the 1970s and 1980s, diversified agriculture was expanding. In the past decade it has been in retreat, even though more land and water are available than ever because of plantation closures. The number of acres in diversified agriculture has dropped about 20 percent the past decade, down to around 40,000 acres.

Much is at stake. When farmland is rezoned, urbanization is nearly irreversible. The land is no longer available for farmers. The best protection of agricultural land is productivity and profitability. Farms that make money are much less in danger of being rezoned. Agriculture in turn virtually guarantees the preservation of open space. Furthermore, agricultural diversification can help communities enjoy greater self-sufficiency, and we can eat healthier foods.

While taro today is a small crop, it symbolizes self-sufficiency.

Beyond concerns for self-sufficiency and fresh food, we need to concentrate on expanding farm exports. We need to put a high priority on University research and development regarding the processing and shipping of selected crops. We will never match the scale of sugar or pineapple, but hopefully we can develop a wider, larger array of products. Some value can be added by the mystique of the words "Made in Hawai'i."

All of this said, it is apparent that diversified agriculture will not usefully fill the lands created by the collapse of plantation agriculture, much as that may be desired. We return to the question, what are we to do with our land?

Housing

Young people ask, "How can we live in Hawai'i if we can't find a place to live?" We need to attack the housing issue with young people in mind. Nothing weakens the continuity of an intergenerational community as much as out-migration, and lack of housing is a big cause. Today we're mostly building housing for older, wealthier people. The question is, how can we develop good "starter" and rental housing reasonably close to centers of employment?

The idea of government leveraging housing developments for a percentage of "affordable" units (often 10 or 20 percent) from developers is no answer, because the costs of the more affordable units are merely distributed to the other buyers.

Let's act more boldly. State government must identify appropriate lands, buy lands, develop infrastructure, hold developers to modest profit margins and help first-time buyers with financing. At the point of sale, the government can recover most of its expenditure.

Home Ownership

Although housing is a huge problem, it is encouraging to observe that in the course of statehood, we have gradually increased home ownership. We have partially closed the gap between the Hawai'i and U.S. averages.

Census	Hawai'i Ownership	U.S. Avg. Ownership	Gap
1960	41%	62%	21%
1970	47%	63%	16%
1980	52%	64%	12%
1990	54%	64%	10%
2000	57%	66%	9%

Urbanization

In spite of the Land Use Law, urban development has tended to take up too much land. As population has doubled, the amount of urban land has increased by two-thirds. That suggests we need to work harder on compact development that preserves open spaces.

Water Supply

Any concept of sustainability must begin with water. A sustainable water supply is simply the level of water use that maintains rather than damages the underground water table.

The state government launched a State Water Commission while I was governor to sustain the water supply. I was alarmed by rapidly increasing water use and by demands to draw down the water lens. We clarified that water is not a commodity to be sold to the highest bidder, but a public resource that must be cared for in the broad public interest over the long term.

The Water Commission brings all types of water use into a single system (for example, public consumers, agriculture and the military). This is important because water use usually draws on the same, or closely related, sources —be they underground aquifers, rivers or reservoirs.

A city or town's demands must be evaluated against the overall supply. Guidelines on distribution of water should be set at arm's length away from City and County governments, because they have a vested interest in development, being financially dependent on property tax.

Hawai'i's parallel system of a State Land Use Commission and a State Water Commission is the right idea. Like sunup and sundown, the use of land and water are related in an endless cycle. When there are proposals for rezoning to urban use, the first thing that should be checked is the water table in that part of the island.

Understanding the water supply, monitoring and protecting it, should be the most fundamental basis of managing growth. We need to be aware that while nature has brilliantly provided most of Hawai'i with water, nonetheless we experience water shortages. We began a system of monitoring the underground aquifers with deep monitoring wells. What we know from monitoring is a work in progress, but clearly some aquifers are being stressed by too much pumping, which results from too much development. The fresh water on top of a given aquifer is falling while the underlying salt water is rising. That is the meaning of "mining" water.

Nonetheless, various forces periodically campaign to abolish the State Water Commission in the name of consolidating government and county home rule. That is folly. The State Water Commission must be maintained and strengthened as a means of protecting water. It is natural and appropriate that there be tension between the State Water Commission, which must preserve water, and the county boards of water supply, which are charged with providing water to consumers.

(For a profile of your monitoring lens, see http://hawaii.gov/dlnr/cwrmt + resources + monitoring data).

Article 11, Section 7. The State has an obligation to protect, control and regulate the use of Hawai'i's water resources for the benefit of its people.

The Economy

As we have seen, plantation agriculture has dropped from being the traditional mainstay of our economy to a modest contributor, while the reverse has occurred with tourism. Let's look a little closer at what happened and why.

Cane Sugar

Hawai'i's cane sugar industry shrank drastically in the mid-1970s as scientists discovered how to convert the natural sugars of corn into the readily consumable sugar called fructose. Around the same time the U.S. Sugar Act was amended to lower the combination of price supports and quotas that made Hawai'i's sugar competitive in a sugar-glutted world market. We could no longer compete against countries that were dumping their subsidized crops for a few cents a pound, a price far below the cost of production.

When the bulk of the Hawai'i sugar industry went down, people were pinching themselves in disbelief.

Pineapple

The second plantation mainstay, pineapple, met a similar fate. Tariffs that had protected the domestic pineapple market were removed, and growers in foreign countries produced at a lower price.

Tourism

Throughout the 50 years of statehood, Hawai'i has rated at or near the top of international surveys on where people most want to visit. In 1958, Hawai'i had 171,588 visitors. In 1959, visitors increased by 42 percent. Eight years later Hawai'i passed the one million mark. During the first decade of statehood, the visitor count increased a whopping 460 percent.

For every visitor in 1959 there are about 30 today.

The growth curve has dipped occasionally, but the overall trend has been steeply upward. Between 1959 and 1973, visitor arrivals grew at an average annual rate over 18 percent. Between 1973 and 1990, the annual growth rate was 5.7 percent. After the 1990s downturn, tourism arrivals increased for several years.

In the process, we became ever more dependent on tourism. We have trouble with slowdowns such as occurred in 2007, and downturns such as occurred in 2008 and 2009 are devastating. The ripple effect touches the entire economy and creates havoc with government revenues and government functions.

Almost certainly tourism will never again grow as it did in the early statehood period. At most the nearly eight million visitors of today are projected to grow by 20 percent over the next quarter century. At the slowest projected growth rate, the curve turns into a nearly flat line.

We can no longer rely economically on the growth of tourism. We must accept that tourism is a mature industry. My attitude is, "Let's make this a blessing in disguise." We can welcome visitors within the constraints of our carrying capacity. We can nurture the aloha spirit.

We can value tourism as a long-term mainstay of our economy. A greatly slowed growth rate fits with our need to guard against overdevelopment and to maintain a clean environment and a relaxed, open exchange with those who come to see Hawai'i. There's nothing more wonderful for visiting families than our people, beaches, water and air. We're not Disneyland and we're not Las Vegas, and we should not try to be. I am opposed to legalized gambling and more generally to development schemes that would turn Hawai'i into an island honky-tonk.

Resource Mining

As we have seen, periods of rapid economic expansion have resulted in an unsustainable "mining" of our most precious resources, land and water. Neither is rapid development good for the workers who are directly involved.

During the past decade, a roughly one-percent annual growth rate has been largely driven by a return to a rapidly growing (and unsustainable) level of construction. The number of construction workers has doubled during the early years of the new century. Young people are being hired into jobs that will not last. Factors such as these surely lie behind the public's preference in surveys for a moderate pace of growth.

Storms and Sea Level

An increase in destructive storms and rising sea levels are closely related threats. Both arise from global warming. Both have serious ecological and economic ramifications for which we must prepare.

The impact of the 1993 Hurricane Iniki on Kaua'i is a vivid example of the power of extreme weather. Many people moved away from Kaua'i and only slowly returned. Infrastructure was so badly damaged that it took tourism eight years to recover to its pre-storm level. Hurricanes and other extreme storms become more likely as a result of global warming.

Similarly, the coming rise in sea levels—resulting from global warming—is a threat both economically and environmentally. As an island state with a long, intricate coastline, depending heavily on our beaches, we should be in the forefront of national and international efforts to minimize global warming.

Warming may seem like an overwhelming trend. Let's shake off our fears and realize there is much we can do. We should adjust zoning and infrastructure projects now to minimize the effects of rising sea levels.

(For the most current science on the effects of sea level rise in Hawai'i see ttp://www.soest.hawaii.edu/coasts/sealevel/NewRates.html)

Energy

An energy shock in 1973 (triggered by the Organization of Petroleum Exporting Countries) set off a wave of alternate energy research and development in Hawai'i. We were—and are—especially vulnerable to oil price increases, because we depend almost totally on oil for all energy forms, including the generation of electricity.

Oil is finite, and we have a responsibility to use it wisely. A range of alternative energy sources are infinite, or practically so. It happens that Hawai'i has a big energy problem, but it has extraordinarily promising solutions, such as solar, biomass, geothermal, wind, wave and ocean thermal. We made promising strides in many of these areas in partnership with the federal government during the 1970s, but most of this work was undermined by national administrations after 1980.

Far-reaching solutions require government research and development. The more sensational possibilities are hydrogen conversion and ocean thermal energy conversion. Other solutions can be approached from the bottom up, household by household and community by community. Each person can become engaged in a combination of energy conservation and alternative energy development. We can all get in the act—in recycling, in the use of solar panels, solar clothes drying, insulation of water heaters and even photovoltaic cells.

Recently the U.S. Department of Energy recognized Hawai'i's potential to be a model in the field of alternate energy. The federal-State agreement focused a stunning economic fact: every 10-percent increase in world oil prices is causing a 0.5-percent reduction in Hawai'i's gross domestic product. That is, we are paying mightily, and will continue to pay, for our dependence on imported oil. As part of the Hawai'i Clean Energy Initiative, the State and federal governments are working cooperatively to generate one fifth of our energy from alternative, renewable sources by the year 2020. While I grant that energy conversion is hard, I say to young people, "Let's push forward. The stakes are high. Let's set high goals."

Alternative energy is finally a national priority. If Hawai'i continues to do its share, alternative energy development is now one of the bright spots in Hawai'i's future.

Leading and Governing

A Globalized World

It is obvious from all the foregoing that most people in Hawai'i went into statehood with high hopes and high expectations. The State government has served us well on many fronts, if not uniformly. Year Fifty is a crossroads. The question of the future is how to mold a State government that is smart and efficient, that cares for what is unique about Hawai'i while navigating our people through an increasingly globalized world.

The Public Good, the Public Commons

Government is about doing together what we cannot do individually. Government must constantly look to its real mission, creating a healthy society: a vibrant economy, a stimulating educational system and a clean environment. It must play a strong role in health care and housing while maintaining a sensible balance with the private sector.

We must value the public commons. Parks are a good example. Our parks are good for us and good for the many visitors who come to enjoy our out-of-doors. Maintenance should be paid for by the general funds of State and local government. The idea of charging people to use parks is philosophically wrong-headed and also self-defeating.

A Sustainable Tax Base

For government to be effective, we must protect the tax base and maintain an appropriate stream of revenues. We must live by principles of fair, progressive taxation.

The burden of taxes should be widely shared. Insofar as possible, we should strive to define an optimal level of taxation: that is, a level that is widely regarded as fair to people at all levels of society, a level that can sustain a streamlined but vigorous government while allowing the private sector to thrive.

Taxes should be as predictable as possible. So should revenues. Stability in taxation is a key virtue in both the public and private sectors, because it allows each to make plans with confidence. Revenue and spending should be managed so that government does not often raise or lower taxes, or sharply raise or lower spending.

Budgeting for the Long Term

Revenues fluctuate up and down every four or five years, but fluctuation in our expenditures should be minimized. When revenues are up, we must plan and manage well to avoid drastic spending cuts when revenues decline. Some revenue should be put aside to help stabilize government through the inevitable economic downturns. Because government cannot do everything, hard choices must be made to keep government lean and operating efficiently.

The question to ask about new government spending is not only the cost next year but the cost five or 10 years downstream. Public debt is to be avoided unless a long-term benefit is clear, at which point debt can be treated as an investment in the future.

Create Level Playing Fields for Business

It is not government's job to favor this or that business or pick winners and losers but to create a level playing field for competing businesses.

Government has a legitimate role in seeking to attract new business, but not at the expense of existing businesses. Solid businesses are attracted to good communities. Using extraordinary incentives to lure businesses to resettle can lead to special favor and is therefore fraught with potential unfairness.

Businesses should be left to do their own thing as much as possible. If unfair practices take place, government has the responsibility to step in. If large new businesses come to Hawai'i, government has the right to insist that jobs be made available to Hawai'i's people—not just menial and blue-collar jobs but executive and managerial positions.

Finding Young Leaders

The cumulative picture is sobering and challenging. Under these circumstances, what are we to do? The book *Limits to Growth* said, "How to bring into being a world that is not only sustainable, functional and equitable but also deeply desirable is a question of leadership and ethics and vision and courage, properties not of computer models but of the human heart and soul."

We need a new wave of smart young leadership. We need it not only in government but in all sectors. We need individuals to lead in their places, by rigorous thinking and by example.

In the period leading up to statehood, I think our society was more actively involved in developing young leaders. Youth legislatures, camps, the YMCA and YWCA, the Young Buddhist Association, Palama Settlement, The Boys Club and Girls Club, Boy Scouts and Girl Scouts were conscious of leadership development. The progressive education programs of some of our public schools were training camps in democratic participation. World War II demanded a great depth and breadth of leadership in Hawai'i. Wide service in wartime, combined with the GI bill of education afterward, amounted to a massive exercise in leadership development.

People ask me, "Why can we not act with the vigor of the earlier years of statehood?" To that I say we can and we must. Time does not stand still. Each period of history has its own possibilities and challenges.

We need young people to step forward, develop their voices, organize around broad themes and lead the way.

Today we have some encouraging initiatives. The Polynesian Voyaging Society continuously develops leaders. We have Hawaiian projects such as the Cultural Learning Center at Kaʻala and rural projects such as Maʻo Organic Farms, which is dedicated to training young people while expanding the practice of organic farming.

The founding members of a new group, Kanu Hawaiʻi, began by asking, "What do we love about Hawaiʻi?" Their second question was, "What concerns us about the future?" Third, "What can we do about it?" With a heavy emphasis on ecology, Kanu asks its members—now in the thousands—to make specific commitments to lead by example. It encourages networking on the job, in institutions or through affinity groups. It is trying to develop leadership in every sector from the grassroots up (see www.kanuhawaii.org).

A vibrant society trains new generations of leaders. Let's do it consciously. Let's equip young people to lead the way to a promising future.

Sustainability Redefines Leadership

People who have genuinely thought about the future will convey a sense of what will be good for coming generations. When something is achieved, to paraphrase the Chinese philosopher Lao Tzu, all involved should feel, "We did this ourselves." When things do not go well, a good leader will try to avoid casting blame, because blame is the surest way to alienate people.

My immigrant father, Ryozo Ariyoshi, summarized his social views with the Japanese phrase *okage sama de*. This phrase describes the intimacy and complexity of human relationships. *Kage* means, literally, "shadow." It means because of your presence, because of your shadow that falls on me, I am what I am.

When we put this perception of human interrelatedness to work, we approach one another with respect. Working for real solutions to problems of the future is a humbling task. We may differ on how we go about it, but we will tend to respect all those who are genuinely involved in this work.

Look to Ourselves

As we in Hawai'i struggle to define ourselves for the next 50 years, let's consciously run against the global tide of homogenization and sameness. Our impulse to be distinct can only work if we look to ourselves and value what we see. We must locate ourselves in context of a positive community story.

Hawai'i is the best case for what, optimistically, America might become. However, we did not get to where we are without conscious effort. Modern Hawai'i did not simply happen. My predecessor, John A. Burns, looked at statehood as facilitating the progress of society, individual by individual. Statehood was intended to further open up what had been a top-down society. It was about each person realizing his or her potential.

In my time as governor, I tried to get an ever-wider range of people involved in public life. When I swore in individuals to serve on task forces and commissions, I would give a pep talk in the governor's chambers. "Don't let one or two people dominate your deliberations," I would say. "Every person has something to contribute. Speak up. Be yourselves, and you will do well." That is the same thing I would tell young people today. "Be yourselves. Think for yourselves. Your thoughts are important. Lead us."

Celebrating each person's potential returns us to the heart of the democratic proposition. As Article 1 of our constitution says: "All persons are free by nature and are equal in their inherent and inalienable rights."

Starting Points

In response to the complexities we face, I do not presume to have the answers. The future belongs to the young; they will live it. However, the starting points do seem apparent.

First, given the trends now in motion, it seems obvious that the next 50 years will be different from the past 50 years. The State of Hawai'i must be frugal and compact on the one hand, worthy of trust and decisive on the other. We must pick our initiatives carefully and pursue them tenaciously.

To take up the economic slack of fading agriculture and flattening tourism, we must trust government with the sensitive task of stimulating the economy on diverse and sustainable fronts.

We must constantly strive for clean air, water, oceans and beaches. We need to proactively develop plans for global warming, rising sea levels and extremes of weather.

Education must be number one, now more than ever. Education is truly the great equalizer.

We need to lead on alternative energy.

We need to operate from a strong sense of who we are. Now as before, we are an uncommon society. We are special.